A Collection of Adventure Stories and Poems in Faith

MARCELLUS MOSLEY

ISBN 979-8-89243-301-3 (hardcover)
ISBN 979-8-89243-302-0 (digital)

Copyright © 2024 by Marcellus Mosley

All rights reserved. No part of this publication may be reproduced, distributed, or transmitted in any form or by any means, including photocopying, recording, or other electronic or mechanical methods without the prior written permission of the publisher. For permission requests, solicit the publisher via the address below.

Christian Faith Publishing
832 Park Avenue
Meadville, PA 16335
www.christianfaithpublishing.com

Printed in the United States of America

To our grandchildren

The Mysterious Arctic Cave

In a land far, far south called Antarctica, there lived a group of animal friends. Among them were a brave snow fox, a curious arctic seal, and a young polar bear who was always hungry. The fox loved adventures, the polar bear had a big appetite, and the seal enjoyed exploring the open sea under the ice.

One day, the fox discovered an amazing cave. However, the cave seemed too dark and cold for the fox alone to venture far inside. Wondering about the source of the constant strong winds, the fox asked the polar bear for help. The polar bear suggested exploring the cave to find answers, but first, they needed to get their friend, the seal, on board. Despite knowing that the seal didn't like to be out of the sea for long, they hoped he would join them.

As they journeyed across the snowy tundra, they thought they spotted their friend, the seal, in the distance. Excitedly calling out to him, they realized it was not him and continued their way toward the Bering Sea. Suddenly, their seal friend jumped out of

the water onto the icy edge. The friends shared their discovery of the mysterious cave with the seal, who was eager to join their exploration.

Little did they know that an aggressive large male polar bear was watching from afar. He had heard them calling for their little seal friend. This polar bear was known for attacking and sometimes devouring seals, foxes, and young polar bears like their friend. You see, male polar bears sometimes will attack young polar bears to eliminate the competition for food. Realizing the danger, the young polar bear knew they had to reach the cave quickly to escape. With the old polar bear chasing them, they hurried toward the cave entrance, fearing they would be trapped. The little white fox had an idea, something that his mother had taught him.

He said to his friends, "Make loud noises by growling, snorting, and I will howl."

"But why?" his friends asked. "Won't that just allow the old polar bear to find us more easily?"

"Just trust me," said the fox.

Just as the old polar bear was about to enter the cave, the three friends made a cacophony of noises—growling, snorting, and howling.

The noise served its purpose as a pile of snow from the cave's roof collapsed, blocking the entrance and keeping the old polar bear out. They were relieved to have escaped. The fox understood that avalanches could be triggered by making lots of noises and vibrations, a lesson the little fox had learned from his mother. They were thankful that the fox's mom had taught him that useful tip.

Inside the cave, it was dark due to the blocked entrance. Luckily, the fox had excellent night vision, so they followed him as he could see fairly well in the darkness. While venturing deeper into the cave, the wind grew stronger, and it became colder. The seal began to worry that they might be trapped. As they continued walking, the young polar bear suggested taking a pause to pray for guidance. They said a prayer, thanking God for saving them from the old polar bear.

Pressing on, they suddenly found a part of the cave where the roof opened to the outside, letting in light and an extremely cold breeze. The fox came up with an idea—to search for footholds on the cave walls that could lead them to the opening. They began climbing, with the seal going first as the polar bear and fox helped him with their strength.

Finally, near the top, they could hear the sound of footsteps outside. Worried that it might be the old polar bear still searching for them, the seal poked his head out cautiously. To their surprise, it was not the old polar bear but the young polar bear's mom. She had been out looking for them.

Suddenly, the old polar bear appeared and climbed on top from beneath the cave's mouth and charged toward them. The mother bear positioned herself over the hole, between the little cub and his friends and the charging old male bear, seemingly ready to fight. Confused, the young polar bear asked his mother what she was doing. She calmly told him to trust her. As the old polar bear jumped into the air to strike, the mother bear swiftly moved, causing the old bear to fall through the hole and into the cave, trapping him there.

They were all amazed and relieved by the clever trick the mother bear had played on the aggressive old bear. They were all safe.

Now the young polar bear had still not eaten anything and said to his mom, "Can we all go back to our cave and have lunch?"

The mother polar bear said, "Absolutely. That's why I was searching for you. I knew you would be hungry."

So they all set off for home, laughing and discussing the great adventure they had exploring the mysterious cave. The mother polar bear also took the opportunity to remind the little seal, the fox, and her own little cub about the truth of God's love for them. She reminded them of the scripture from the Bible:

> He will call on me, and I will answer him;
> I will be with him in trouble,

I will deliver him and honor him.

With long life I will satisfy him

and show him my salvation.

The young friends became very quiet and thought about what the mother polar bear had said to them all the way home. They were thankful.

The End

Written by Marcellus Mosley

October 24, 2023

Parent/adult discussion with the child/children

New words learned. Name and discuss three.

1.

2.

3.

The morals of the story. Describe and discuss three.

1.

2.

3.

Following Jesus, Winning with Grace and Mercy

A story for Aubrey and Ava

Once upon a time, in a small town nestled among rolling hills, there were two little girls named Emma and Lily. From a young age, they learned to love Jesus and follow His teachings. They attended a local school where kindness and empathy were not always priorities for everyone.

Emma and Lily, filled with the love of Jesus in their hearts, approached each day with joy and compassion. They greeted their classmates with smiles and tried to befriend everyone, including the little boys who sometimes treated them harshly. Despite the hurtful words and actions, the girls remembered the lessons of their faith: to love those who despise you and mistreat you.

One sunny morning, as Emma and Lily walked through the school gate, they saw a group of boys huddled together, whispering and laughing. The girls knew they were the target of

their meanness, as they had witnessed it before. However, instead of retaliating or seeking revenge, the girls decided to respond to these challenges with grace and mercy.

Throughout the day, the boys continued to taunt Emma and Lily, making unkind remarks and mocking their beliefs. But the girls remained steadfast in their faith, finding strength in the teachings of Jesus. During lunch break, when the boys knocked over their trays, the girls smiled and helped clean up the mess, showing kindness in return.

Outside the schoolyard, there was a beautiful garden where Emma and Lily liked to spend their free time. They found solace among the colorful flowers and fresh air, praying for guidance and strength. One day, while they were enjoying a quiet moment in the garden, a new boy named Ben came up to them. Ben had always watched how the girls handled themselves in school and was amazed by their unwavering grace.

Curiosity sparked within Ben, and he asked Emma and Lily why they responded to the boys' cruelty with such kindness. The girls shared stories from the Bible about Jesus's teachings on loving others, even those who harm you. They explained that by showing grace and forgiveness, they hoped to make a difference in the boys' lives.

Ben was touched by their words, moved by the girls' unwavering faith. He asked if they could join in spreading kindness together. Emma, Lily, and Ben became an unlikely trio, spreading love and treating others with compassion wherever they went. Their acts of grace began to soften the hearts of the boys who had once treated them harshly.

As time passed, the boys started to question their own actions, realizing the value of empathy and respect. They witnessed the transformation within Emma, Lily, and Ben and felt inspired to change their ways. Slowly but surely, the girls' response of love and kindness began to influence those who once despised them, creating a ripple effect of compassion within the school.

Emma's and Lily's unwavering faith and reliance on Jesus's teachings had a profound impact on their school community. The harsh treatment from the boys became a thing of the past as the power of grace and mercy prevailed. The school became a place where love, understanding, and acceptance thrived.

And so Emma and Lily continued to spread Jesus's teachings of love and forgiveness, making a lasting impact on their school and beyond. Their story became an inspiring tale, cherished by everyone who encountered it, reminding people that even in the face of difficulty, responding with grace and mercy can create a world filled with love and understanding.

The End

September 15, 2023

Written by Marcellus Mosley

Parent/adult discussion with the child/children

New words learned. Name and discuss three.

1.

2.

3.

The morals of the story. Describe and discuss three.

1.

2.

3.

The Adventure of Hannah and Naomi

The Faithful Father

Once upon a time, there were two little girls named Hannah and Naomi. Hannah was a very artistic and outgoing girl, while Naomi was more soft-spoken and creative. Both of them loved Jesus and wanted their lives to reflect His love toward others. One day, they went on a hiking trip in the wilderness. The air was crisp and cool, a pleasant change from their home in Texas. As they ventured deeper into the woods, they enjoyed the beautiful sounds of birds chirping, leaves rustling in the wind, and the blue sky filled with fluffy clouds.

While hiking up the mountain, they came across a steep cliff that dropped down dramatically into a ravine. Naomi, being cautious, warned Hannah to stay away from the edge. But Hannah, being bold and curious, insisted on seeing what was down there. She walked right up to the edge of the cliff, unknowingly causing the rocks beneath her feet to crumble. The edge of the cliff slowly gave way, and Hannah found herself hanging on to a small limb that grew from inside the rock. Panicking, she called out for help.

Back at the family cabin on the other side of the mountain, their parents started to worry. Hannah and Naomi's father grabbed his flashlight and set out to find the girls, who had been gone for hours. As the sun began to set, his worry grew, and he decided to stop and pray for guidance. After the prayer, he ran even faster, desperate to find his little girls. Darkness descended upon the mountain, making the search more challenging. Finally, the father reached the peak of the mountain and called out frantically, but there was no reply.

Meanwhile, Naomi had grabbed a vine and was trying to lower it down to Hannah. "Grab the vine, Hannah!" she cried out.

But Hannah's arms were too short, and she couldn't reach it. Realizing they needed help, she urged Naomi to go find their father quickly. Just as Naomi left, their father heard Hannah's desperate cry for help. He ran as fast as he could toward the sound, stumbling over rocks and branches in the dark. When he reached the edge of the mountain, Naomi informed her father about the situation. With determination, the father took the vine from Naomi and managed to reach Hannah. He pulled her up to safety.

With tears of joy streaming down their faces, the father hugged his two daughters tightly. On their way back home, the girls asked their father how he found them in the dark. The father shared that he had no idea where they were, so he stopped and prayed to Jesus for guidance. The girls were intrigued and asked if Jesus had helped him find them. Quoting from the book of Jeremiah, the father explained how God promises to reveal hidden things to those who call upon Him. He believed that God had indeed shown him the way to find his girls. Overwhelmed with gratitude, they stopped and said a prayer of thanks for their safe rescue.

And so this great adventure of Hannah and Naomi taught them about the faithfulness of their father and the power of prayer. As they returned home, they carried with them a testimony of God's love and protection. They were forever grateful for their father's unwavering faith and trust in God.

The End

October 6, 2023

Written by Marcellus Mosley

Parent/adult discussion with the child/children

New words learned. Name and discuss three.

1.

2.

3.

The morals of the story. Describe and discuss three.

1.

2.

3.

My Mountain Escape

Mom and I decided to take a trip to the mountains. It was a beautiful day, with crisp but sunny air, as usual here in Colorado. We had chosen to hike together to the peak of one of the most scenic mountains in the Denver area. Since we were only going for a few hours, we packed a couple bottles of water, some crackers, and cheese as a snack. We let Dad know that we would be back soon, as he was working out in our garage as usual. You see, my dad is very big and strong. Some of my friends even call him the Hulk.

So Mom and I loaded up the jeep and headed to the mountains, full of excitement. We laughed all the way up there. My mom is sweet and funny and makes me feel warm all over. She told me stories of when she and my dad first started dating, the trips they took together all over the world before they got married, about our first house, and how we came to live in the house we now live in. Their journey together had been so much fun even before I came along. Of course, it's even more fun now that I'm here.

At approximately 11:00 a.m., we arrived at the base of the mountain. The day was still beautiful, with a slight breeze, but you could tell in the air that it was a bit chilly. We took out our snacks, put on our hiking boots, and began our ascent up the mountain. It was October, and this time of year, while beautiful, often brings unpredictable weather changes. So Mom brought her cell phone just in case. We crossed a beautiful meadow at the base of the mountain, with a huge tree that had to be three or four hundred years old, its branches stretching out like an old man's arms reaching for the sky. We stopped there and took a photo together before continuing up the trail. A well-built, though small, little bridge crossed a beautiful babbling stream, and to our surprise, we saw river otters playfully fishing with their young ones. They were so fast and graceful in the water; it was mesmerizing to watch. I wanted to stay and watch them and have a snack there, but Mom said, "Let's keep moving. The day is going to get away from us, Hudson." So we continued our trek.

The mountains in Colorado are majestic, especially this time of year, with their white snowcapped peaks glistening in the sun. We were gradually gaining altitude, with Denver being six thousand feet in elevation and us climbing another one thousand feet. As a result, the mountain air started to get quite chilly. But Mom came prepared—she pulled out one of my winter jackets

from her backpack and a sweater for herself, and we continued our hike. Mom loves to sing to me, but on this tough section of the trail, she simply hummed one of my favorite Sunday school tunes, "Our God is an awesome God."

By 2:00 p.m., Mom and I reached the summit, but we were out of breath. Just then, Dad called, surprising us since he had business calls until 5:00 p.m. on Mondays. Mom's face looked worried, and I knew something was not right.

After hanging up, she said, "Hudson, we have to get down the mountain quickly. Dad said there is a storm coming in. Don't worry, son."

She assured me that if we left now, we should reach the jeep before the storm arrived. So we packed up and hurried down the mountain. The skies turned dark and ominous, with lightning flashing in the distance and thunder roaring. Mom urged us to jog carefully, but after only running about one hundred yards, the snow began falling so heavily that we couldn't see in front of us. Mom said we had to find cover, so we searched for the little cave we had noticed right before reaching the summit. Thankfully, we found it and ran inside.

Mom took out her cell phone to call Dad and inform him that we would be waiting out the storm in the cave. I could hear Dad's voice through the phone saying, "Stay there. I'm on my way." Mom had informed Dad of what route we were planning to take to the summit.

The view from our vantage point was breathtaking. We could see for miles, although the scenery was blanketed in snow. Mom tried to lift my spirits by suggesting we sing one of my favorite tunes. I agreed, and we began singing, "It Is Well with My Soul." Surprisingly, it worked. The song distracted our minds from the potential danger outside, particularly the verse that goes,

> *Through many dangers, toils, and snares,*
> *I have already come.*
> *This grace that brought me safe thus far,*
> *and grace will lead me home.*

In addition to knowing that Dad was on his way, I also knew that the Hulk would be arriving soon. However, little did we realize that the snow was heavier at the base and had started falling before we even noticed it coming down. As the sun began to fade through the heavy snow, we both started shivering uncontrollably. Mom suggested that we huddle together to share body heat and keep warm. She was right, as always, because we instantly felt warmer as she held me tightly. Suddenly, a faint noise echoed from below the mountain, gradually growing louder. We initially mistook it for Dad's voice and called out to him. But as the noise approached, we realized it wasn't human—it sounded like a big cat. Nervously, I asked Mom if it was a mountain lion.

She replied, "I think it might be Hudson, so let's remain quiet and stop calling out."

Darkness enveloped us, and fear gripped me, causing trembles that were not solely due to the cold. We could hear the big cat prowling around, sometimes above us, sometimes to the side, and sometimes below. Mom searched the cave for a rock or stick but found nothing. She suggested we pray, asking God for divine protection and safety. At that very moment, we heard the sound of heavy footsteps crunching through the snow. Mom instructed me to stay quiet and, cautiously, stepped outside the cave.

She peered down the mountain and called out, "Travis!"

The relief was palpable when Dad's voice responded. I was no longer afraid or shivering. I tried to run out of the cave, but Mom quickly pushed me back inside and insisted that I stay. After about fifteen minutes, thanks to the deep snow, Dad finally arrived. At that moment, I knew everything would be alright. God had answered our prayers. We no longer heard the growls of the big cat that had been near us, and I assumed that the Hulk must have scared it away.

My parents had camped in the mountains many times before I was born, and Dad had brought his backpack, which seemingly had sleeping bags tied to it. Dad informed us that we would have to spend the night as the snow had become too deep, and it was impossible to see the way down, even with a flashlight. He assured us that he had brought our heaviest sleeping bags and that we would all snuggle together to keep warm until morning. So we climbed into the sleeping-bags together, taking off our shoes first, and zipped it up over our heads. Mom shared another story from the Bible, and before long, I was fast asleep nestled between my parents.

The following morning, the skies were clear, the sun was shining, and the snow was beginning to melt away. We made our way down the mountain, and by ten o'clock, we were in our jeeps, heading home. On the journey, Mom reminded me and Dad that God answers prayers. He had heard our prayer on the mountain and had sent Dad with all the necessary supplies to get us through the night. We all expressed our gratitude and agreed the next time we decide to take a mountain trip, we will make sure the Hulk is with us.

The End

Written by Marcellus Mosley

Parent/adult discussion with the child/children

New words learned. Name and discuss three.

1.

2.

3.

The morals of the story. Describe and discuss three.

1.

2.

3.

My Family Adventure in Africa

In December 2023, my family embarked on an incredible trip to Africa with my parents and grandparents. It turned out to be the most thrilling, yet dangerous, journey I have ever experienced. My little sister, Ava, who is five years old, and I, Aubrey, were beyond excited about the trip. Our grandparents, Lolli and Pop, had gifted us with a trip to Africa for Christmas 2023. We had always been fascinated by the African savanna, thanks to watching the Discovery Channel with our parents and grandparents. We were captivated by the elephants, hippos, and especially the majestic lions. However, we didn't have much love for the hyenas, who always seemed to steal from weaker animals like the cheetah. Nonetheless, we understood their importance in the ecosystem. Little did we know that our adventure would involve an unforgettable encounter.

On our first day, we arrived at a small village with a lodge that had a rustic appearance. However, once we stepped inside, we

were amazed by the beautiful natural wood finishes made from acacia trees. The lodge had traditional thatched roofs, and the interior felt like a majestic palace to my sister and me. We were served exotic foods that we had never tasted before, including antelope and water buffalo steaks. Everything was delicious.

The following day, our guide, Mombasa, took us on our first safari in an open-cab Land Rover. Before we set off, Mombasa emphasized the importance of safety, instructing us to keep our arms and legs inside the jeep at all times. We also noticed a man carrying a rifle or machine gun–type weapon. Curious, I asked Mombasa why he had that weapon. He explained that the man was there to provide protection and ensure our safety but assured us that nothing would go wrong. With that, we climbed into the Land Rover, filled with excitement to see the animals in the plains.

It didn't take long for us to spot a giraffe, and Mombasa asked us to grab our binoculars. We watched in awe as a mother giraffe gave birth right before our eyes. The baby struggled to stand on its wobbly legs, and despite the mother's long neck preventing her from assisting, the little one managed to stand up. We were mesmerized by this incredible sight for about an hour. Even Lolli, our grandmother, was moved to tears. It was an emotional moment for our family, and it was only the beginning of our trip.

Ava began to feel hungry, so we snacked on the apples and peanut butter and honey sandwiches that Mom had packed, despite Ava's peanut allergy. The sandwich used a kind of butter that tasted like peanuts. With our hunger satisfied, Mombasa decided it was time to continue our safari and explore more of the wildlife in the reserve. The road was bumpy and dusty, with no concrete or asphalt in sight. We bounced around in the open jeep for hours, but it was all worth it. Eventually, we came across two young cheetahs with their mother. The mother cheetah appeared focused on something, and we soon understood why. Mombasa enlightened us, telling us she was hunting down antelopes. Without any hesitation, the mother cheetah dashed off with incredible speed, catching one of the antelopes by the neck. We watched in awe as the cheetah's cubs joined in for a meal. It felt like a scene straight out of the Discovery Channel. The thrill made Dad take out his iPhone and start recording the event. I called out to Mom and Lolli, urging them to come see. However, Mombasa reminded us to prioritize safety and keep our arms and legs inside the jeep at all times.

Dad and Pop couldn't resist getting closer to the kill to capture better footage despite Mombasa's agitation. Mom and Lolli pleaded with Pop and Dad, begging them not to go any farther as it was dangerous. Pop reassured us, telling Mom and Lolli to

stay in the jeep and promising that everything would be okay. However, the tension in the air was palpable, and Mom's and Lolli's agitation was becoming more evident by the minute.

As my dad and Pop continued to capture amazing shots of the cheetah kill, the adrenaline of the moment took over, and we temporarily forgot about the potential danger lurking on the African plains. Mom and Lolli, however, remained vigilant and made sure that Ava and I stayed safely inside the jeep.

Suddenly, out of nowhere, a lioness emerged from the brush. Its sudden appearance startled everyone, and Mom screamed for Dad to come back as she screamed that there was a lion. But it was already too late. The lioness had closed the distance to the kill in the blink of an eye. Dad and Pop had to act quickly, scrambling up a nearby tree for safety.

The growls of the lioness resonated ominously as she stared up at Pop and Dad, still perched atop the tree. I could see at that moment Dad and Pop had their eyes raised to heaven, praying. My heart raced as I watched them desperately clinging to the branches, desperate for an escape. It was at this moment that we heard a strange howl, and all of us turned our attention toward the south.

To our astonishment, a pack of hyenas came rushing toward the carcass, their presence distracting the lioness from her attack on Pop and Dad. She now focused on defending her kill from these intruders. The hyenas relentlessly swarmed the carcass, engaging in a fierce battle with the lioness.

Despite being outnumbered, the lioness fought valiantly. The scene unfolded before our eyes, and the tension in the air was so thick you could cut it with a knife. Eventually, the hyenas managed to chase the lioness away, claiming their victory over the carcass. And with the hyena horde satisfied, Pop and Dad were finally safe to descend from the tree, their prayers for rescue and protection answered.

As they stood on the ground, looking at the cleaned carcass, Pop mentioned how the intervention of the hyenas had saved them all. Dad added that if it hadn't been for those hyenas, the lioness might have succeeded in her attack. It was a humbling moment as we reflected on the power of prayer and the protection we had been granted.

On the drive back to the lodge, Pop shared how, as they were clinging to the tree and praying for deliverance, a profound calm and peace had washed over both him and Dad. They knew deep down that everything would be alright, as they put their trust in the Lord.

That night, as we gathered for dinner at the lodge, I couldn't help but say a prayer from *Psalm 91:14–15, "'Because he loves* me,' says the L*ord*, 'I will rescue him; I will protect him, for he acknowledges my name. He will call on me, and I will answer him; I will be with him in trouble.'"* It has become one of my favorite psalms, holding a special place in my heart after this incredible experience.

And you know what? From that day forward, our favorite African animal became the hyena. We marveled at how God had used those seemingly ominous creatures to save my dad and my Pop, reminding us that He works in mysterious and miraculous ways.

The End

Written by Marcellus Mosley

October 9, 2023

Parent/adult discussion with the child/children

New words learned. Name and discuss three.

1.

2.

3.

The morals of the story. Describe and discuss three.

1.

2.

3.

A Poem to Aubrey and Ava

Pop and Lolli love you, and believe it, for sure we do.

If anyone asks you, just tell them, "Yes, it's true."

We love holding you both close and tight.

And squeeze you both with all our might.

If we could pick from the globe just two little girls.

It would be both of you from anyone else in this world.

We pray earnestly for you both day and night.

That God would bless you and give you real sight.

That you might clearly see Him as a savior to love.

And be fully assured He will take you to live with Him forever and ever up above.

God is your strength and the power in your might.

He empowers you both to truly love and shine forever bright.

Be good little ones and give Him your praise.

For He is your father in this life and for all your days.

I tell you be full of joy and forever be happy.

Knowing you're also loved dearly by Lolli and your old Poppi.

Ava and Aubrey, I sing you this little song.

To remind you that heaven is your true home.

Written by Marcellus Mosley

(September 21, 2021)

A Poem for Hudson
by Marcellus Mosley

Today, a son was born into this world

With cries of joy, he unfurled

A new life now begins to unfold

As his tiny fingers tightly hold

His parents' hearts are full of love

As they gaze upon this gift from above

Their world now forever changed

A new chapter in their lives arranged

May this little one grow in strength and grace

And always have a smile on his face

May his life be filled with wonder and joy

And find happiness that nothing can destroy

On this day of his birth, let us rejoice

A new life to be treasured and embraced with poise

We welcome this little bundle of joy

And wish him a life that's blessed and full of employ.

Written by Marcellus Mosley

About the Author

Marcellus Mosley, a gifted Christian author born and raised in the Midwest, now hailing from Texas, has had a fascinating journey in life. Raised in a Christian home with seven wonderful siblings, he imbibed the teachings of his faith from his parents. Marcellus went on to embark on a successful business career in Texas, ultimately reaching the pinnacle of his career in the role of chief operating officer in the real estate industry. Despite retiring from a fulfilling forty-three-year career in business at the age of sixty-three in 2023, Marcellus felt a persistent yearning to contribute further to the world with the strong sense that God was not quite done with him yet.

With pen and paper in hand, Marcellus began to document the captivating stories he had often created and shared with his beloved grandchildren. Encouraged by his wife and children, he took the courageous step of submitting his writings to a renowned Christian publishing company. Marcellus's writing style masterfully blends adventure with principled morals drawn from the timeless teachings of the Bible. This unique approach not only captivates young readers but also imparts valuable life lessons in an entertaining manner.

Marcellus's mission is twofold: to introduce Jesus to children unfamiliar with Him and to strengthen the faith of those who already know Him. His heartfelt desire is to bring glory to the name of Jesus through his writings, allowing readers to experience divine joy in His name.

Through his creative works, Marcellus Mosley aims to inspire, instruct, and entertain young minds, leaving an indelible impact on their lives. With his unwavering passion and dedication, he strives toward the noble goal of awakening the hearts of children to the transformative power of faith.

A Poem to Aubrey and Ava

Pop and Lolli love you, and believe it, for sure we do.

If anyone asks you, just tell them, "Yes, it's true."

We love holding you both close and tight.

And squeeze you both with all our might.

If we could pick from the globe just two little girls.

It would be both of you from anyone else in this world.

We pray earnestly for you both day and night.

That God would bless you and give you real sight.

That you might clearly see Him as a savior to love.

And be fully assured He will take you to live with Him forever and ever up above.

God is your strength and the power in your might.

He empowers you both to truly love and shine forever bright.

Be good little ones and give Him your praise.

For He is your father in this life and for all your days.

I tell you be full of joy and forever be happy.

Knowing you're also loved dearly by Lolli and your old Poppi.

Ava and Aubrey, I sing you this little song.

To remind you that heaven is your true home.

Written by Marcellus Mosley

(September 21, 2021)